#JustMyThoughts

THE INTRO:

I Never Did Appreciate
LION To Myself
. . .
Be Attentive
To Your Experiences
With GRATITUDE
. . .

— Novah's Son

COPYRIGHT© | FAITHFUL SENSE™

#JustMyThoughts

EXPERIENCE
&
EMBRACE LIFE
—
TWO THINGS WE DON'T DO.
SIMPLY,
BECAUSE WE DO
NOT ALLOW OURSELVES THE
SPACE & OPPORTUNITY TO.
—
WE AS A PEOPLE WERE
"TAUGHT" TO THRIVE IN
CHAOS! DISCORD!
REVOLT IN ANGER & JUDGEMENT.
—
FORGETTING THAT WE WERE
ALL BORN IN THE SAME
WHOLENESS.
ACCEPTANCE.
AND
COMPASSION.
AS
—
UNCONDITIONAL LOVE
. . .
LET'S ENGAGE OUR MIND,
LET'S EMPOWER OUR HEARTS,
REINTRODUCE SPIRIT
TO THE MINDFULNESS OF YOUR
. . .

ESSENCE

DATE

DATE

#JustMyThoughts

TO WHOM IT MAY CONCERN:
(FOR THE GUILTY CONSCIOUS ONLY)
-
I WASN'T TRYING TO TEAR DOWN YA LIL "WALL"
& I WASN'T GON LET, ASK, NOR FORCE
YOU TO BREAK THROUGH MINES.
-
SO EXCUSE ME FOR WANTING
TO BYPASS THE EMOTIONALLY DISTURBED!
-
I JUST THOUGHT WE COULD CLIMB UP
THE MOUNTAIN OF OUR OWN
INDISCRETIONS WILLINGLY.
MEET EACH OTHER AT THE TOP.
RELAX OUR HEARTS & MINDS
TO THE SAME FREQUENCY.
& THEN BUILD IN EACH OTHERS PRESENCE
TO ENJOY THE SUNRISE TOGETHER.
I MEAN, CONFIDENCE & COMFORT
SOUNDED GOOD TO ME!
BUT WHAT TOO MUCH? (MAYBE)
NOT ENOUGH? (LATELY)
NO TOLERANCE OR TRUST FOR SELF? (DEBATE ME)
OR
WERE YOU JUST FRONTIN' LIKE THE REST,
BUMPIN' YA GUMS, TRYIN TO GIT YA TONGUE WET?
(SOUNDS A LIL SHADY)
WELPERSSS I GUESS...
-
DAMN ANOTHER ONE BITES THE FRUIT.
#TRUSTISSUES

TRULY WANTED TO BE YOURS

Sacred In My Purpose.

DATE

DATE

#JustMyThoughts

FORTUNATELY,
I WAS EXPOSED TO
REAL ISSUES,
THEREFORE I UNDERSTAND.

-

MORE THAN I EVER
WANTED TO BEFORE
&
WHEN I EVER
NEEDED TO.

-

HENCE THE MAIN REASON
I'M DISCERNED & NAUSEATED
BY THE NEGATIVITY
OF YA BULL
YET REFINED WITH THE POSITIVITY
THAT REFLECTS
MY SAVVY "TUDE"

#YOULIVE&YOULEARN.EDU

Sacred In My Truth.

COPYRIGHT© | FAITHFUL SENSE™

DATE

#JustMyThoughts

I'LL CALL HER
—

A "B", IF SHE RESPONDS TO QUICK WITH RECKLESS EMOTION.

A TRUE FRIEND, IF SHE RESPECTS THE UNSOLICITED NOTION.

A SIMPLE LITTLE GIRL, IF SHE DEPENDS ON BEING NUMB.

A COURAGEOUS BEING, IF SHE DREAMS & LIVES AS ONE.

A GENTLE HEART, IF HER MIND & BODY ENAMORS IT.

A WORTHY WIFE, IF SHE RIDES & DIES BY IT.

A NATURAL BEAUTY, IF HER INSTINCTS PREACH FAITH.

MY SOUL, IF SHE TRUSTS ME WITH HERS GIVE & TAKE.

AND MY "W.O.M.A.N"

THAT DESERVES TO BE LOVED AS SHE
CAN DECIPHER THE DIFFERENCE!
KEEPING HER SHIT TOGETHER IN COMFORT.
WITH CONFIDENCE.
NO MATTER THE SITUATION.
NOR PLACE.

Sacred Amongst All Others.

COPYRIGHT© | FAITHFUL SENSE™

DATE

DATE

#JustMyThoughts

"... WHEN ONE LEAVES THE METHOD
TO EXAMINES THE MOTIVE,
THE CAREFULLY STACKED BLOCKS
OF LOGIC BEGIN TO TUMBLE.

—

THAT TYPE OF LOVE ISN'T LOGICAL;
IT CAN'T BE NEATLY OUTLINED IN A SERMON
OR EXPLAINED IN A TERM PAPER

...

IT IS INEXPLICABLE.
IT DOESN'T HAVE A DROP OF LOGIC
NOR A THREAD OF RATIONALITY.

—

AND YET, IT IS THAT VERY IRRATIONALITY
THAT GIVES THE GOSPEL IT'S GREATEST DEFENSE.
FOR ONLY GOD COULD LOVE LIKE THAT ..."
- MAX LUCADO
GOD CAME NEAR

THE EQUATION OF HUMANITY = BE-ING
THE WILLINGNESS OF
THAT NATURE TO LOVE!

Divinely Guided & Protected.

COPYRIGHT© | FAITHFUL SENSE™

DATE

#JustMyThoughts

YOU LIVE, YOU LEARN.
YOU LOVE, YOU LEARN.
YOU CRY, YOU LEARN.
YOU LOSE, YOU LEARN.
YOU BLEED, YOU LEARN.
YOU SCREAM, YOU LEARN.
YOU GRIEVE, YOU LEARN.
YOU CHOKE, YOU LEARN.
YOU LAUGH, YOU LEARN.
YOU CHOOSE, YOU LEARN.
YOU PRAY, YOU LEARN.
YOU ASK, YOU LEARN.
YOU LIVE, YOU LEARN.
-
ALANIS MORISSETTE WROTE
ONE HELL OF A SONG...

Grounded To Earth.

COPYRIGHT© | FAITHFUL SENSE™

DATE

DATE

#JustMyThoughts

THE

SHADOW

—

MUST NOT

"DEPEND"

TO PROTECT.

—

BUT

—

PRESENT

TO HEAL.

*SINCERELY,
THE LIGHT WITHIN*

Sacred In My Purpose.

COPYRIGHT© | FAITHFUL SENSE™

DATE

DATE

#JustMyThoughts

THE STORY I TELL TO THE ONE
INTERESTED ENOUGH TO SIT ME DOWN
AND STRADDLE ME WITH WARM ARMS
TO LISTEN WITH UNDERSTANDING
WILL COURAGEOUSLY BE THE ONE
I'M WILLING TO SUBMIT TO
WITHOUT CAUTION...

SHOW ME STRENGTH TO LISTEN,
I'LL SHARE COURAGE TO SPEAK!

#TAKENOTE

I AM
THE INFINITE ONE

Sacred In My Truth.

DATE

DATE

#JustMyThoughts

TO SOLVE
THE EQUATION OF HUMANITY:
◻
AS BE-ING(S) WE MUST,

. . .

ADD (+) | UNCONDITIONAL LOVE
SUBTRACT (−) | ALL WE BLAME AS HATE
MULTIPLY (X) | GOODNESS & GRACE
& STOP THE UNNECESSARY
DIVIDE (/) | BETWEEN TRUTH & EXPERIENCE

. . .

HOW DO YOU CHOOSE TO
SHOW UP IN THE WORLD?

Sacred Amongst All Others.

COPYRIGHT© | FAITHFUL SENSE™

DATE

#JustMyThoughts

LIVE FOR LIFE,
LEARN FROM TRUTH,
EXHALE THROUGH FAITH &
EMBRACE LIGHT AFTER A DEATH

PLEASE SPARE ME
ANTICS WITH
DISCOURAGEMENT
& NEGATIVITY

BLESS EM' FOR
THEY NO NOT...
IT'S A REBIRTH!

Divinely Guided & Protected.

COPYRIGHT© | FAITHFUL SENSE™

DATE

DATE

COPYRIGHT© | FAITHFUL SENSE™

#JustMyThoughts

COLOR ME

—

RED
THE "LIFE" I LIVE WITHOUT FEAR OR REGRET.

ORANGE
THE "HEALING" ENDURED TO STAND AS INNER STRENGTH.

YELLOW
THE "SUNLIGHT" THAT GUIDES MY JOURNEY.

GREEN
ALLOW FLOW IN "NATURE" TO RUN IT'S DESIRED COURSE.

INDIGO
THE "SERENITY" TO ACCEPT, LOVE & TRUST MYSELF.

VIOLET
THE "SPIRIT" & FAITH THAT I INDULGE TO GAIN PEACE.

—

ENACT YOUR WISDOM AS GOD WITH SELF IN ALL SENSES. YOU'LL FIND THE TRUE NATURE OF PEACE, HAPPINESS & LOVE WHEREVER YOUR ESSENSE ARRIVES!

Grounded To Earth.

COPYRIGHT© | FAITHFUL SENSE™

DATE

DATE

#JustMyThoughts

YOU'LL TRANSMUTE ALL THINGS BITTER!
AS YOU TRUST THE STRENGTH OF THE SOUL.
YOU'LL PROBABLY LEARN THE HARD WAY,
YET THE DAYS ARE TOO VALUABLE
& PRECIOUS FOR ME
TO EVEN ACKNOWLEDGE MISERY
LET ALONE ENTERTAIN IT'S COMPANY

.,.

OUT MY FACE, OUT MY ZONE,
OFF MY NEWS FEED WITH THE DISTRACTIONS.

...

DO NOT SPARE ME, SPARE YOUR DAMN SELF.
I KNOW YOU LIKE KISS'N, SUCK'N OR EAT'N ASS,
TO EACH THEIR OWN.
BUT DO SELF THE FAVOR
PULL YOUR HEAD OUT & READ A BOOK!
START IN JOB 3:20,
THEN LINGER IN ROMANS TO 8:38-39
#CALLINYOURLIGHT

Sacred In My Purpose.

COPYRIGHT© | FAITHFUL SENSE™

DATE

DATE

#JustMyThoughts

TELL ME SOMETHING I DON'T <u>KNOW</u>
SHOW ME SOMETHING I'VE NEVER <u>SEEN</u>
SAY SOMETHING YOU DIDN'T MEAN TO <u>SAY</u>
BUT <u>BELIEVE</u>

SIDENOTE:

TRUST GOES A LONG WAY BUT IF YOU DON'T TRUST YOURSELF, HOW YOU GON TRUST SOMEONE OR EXPECT SOMEONE TO TRUST YOU??

#MAKEHISTORY
DON'T REPEAT IT!

Sacred In My Truth.

COPYRIGHT© | FAITHFUL SENSE™

DATE

DATE

#JustMyThoughts

ANYBODY & EVERYBODY
THAT KNOWS "ME",
KNOWS I'VE NEVER
BEEN ONE TO ENTERTAIN.

—

SO WITH THAT KNOWLEDGE,
DON'T ASK ABOUT ME!

—

ASK ME.

—

IT'S ONLY IF I WANT TO,

. . .

I'LL SHOW YOU WHAT
"THEY" TALK ABOUT.

Sacred Amongst All Others.

DATE

DATE

#JustMyThoughts

THAT "NEW YEAR'S DAY"
SOMEONE WISE TOLD ME
THAT "REGARDLESS OF WHATEVER
IN OR OUT YOUR LIFE
THOSE THAT HONESTLY LOVED
& GENUINELY CARED FOR YOU
WILL NOT ONLY WISH YOU
THE BEST AS SUPPORT
INSIST THE ENERGY TO REMAIN POSITIVE
YET PRAYS FOR UR SUCCESS
WITH ENCOURAGEMENT

...BUT...

IT BEGINS WHEN YOU ACKNOWLEDGE
YOUR WORTH TO ACCEPT IT
BELIEVE IN YOURSELF TO EXCEPT IT
& COMMIT WITH FAITH SO YOU
THRIVE ON YOUR FULL POTENTIAL
ALL THAT SHIT SOUNDED GOOD TO ME!

#WHO'SLISTENING

Divinely Guided & Protected.

COPYRIGHT© | FAITHFUL SENSE™

DATE

DATE

#JustMyThoughts

CALM.

COOL.

&

DAMN I'M MISSING A "C" !?!

WAIT, WAIT, HOL' LUP 2.5

(YIN WALTZ IN & SNUGGLES UP TO YANG)

THERE WE GO .,.,.,.,.,. COLLECTED!

#SAFEKEEPING ☯

Grounded To Earth.

DATE

DATE

#JustMyThoughts

DON'T FOCUS ON THE STORM

THE STORM WILL PASS

PAY ATTENTION TO THE SEED

.

.

BE NURTURING, PLANT YOUR SEEDS.
BE LOVING WITH THEIR GROWTH.
BE GROUNDED, IN ENERGY GIVEN.

.

.

WATER YOUR ROOTS, IN YOUR LIGHT!

Sacred In My Purpose.

DATE

DATE

#JustMyThoughts

I DON'T FALL IN TO FALL OUT!
(F) A BROKEN DREAM,
JUST KNOW I LOVED YOU FOR A REASON
& ONCE YOU GOT IT IT'S CHERISHED,
REGARDLESS OF WHATEVER
& IF I EVER SHOWED IT OR SAID IT
...
TRUST ME, I MEANT IT!
I JUST HAD TO RETURN MY HEART TO SENDER.
AS YOU NO LONGER DESERVED MY AFFECTION.
,.
SHOUTOUT TO THE 1ST OF EVERYTHING,
SHOUTOUT THE ONE THAT GOT CAUGHT UP,
SHOUTOUT TO THE ONE LOCK'D UP, &
SHOUTOUT THE ONE THAT DIDN'T G.A.F

-

I APPRECIATE Y'ALL

...

NO SERIOUSLY, I DO!

Sacred In My Truth.

COPYRIGHT© | FAITHFUL SENSE™

DATE

#JustMyThoughts

I HAVE AN
EVERYDAY RITUAL
THAT WORKS FOR ME!
🕯
ALIGN WITH <u>SELF</u> FIRST,
EVERYTHING ELSE.

.

.

JUST HAPPENS TO FALLS IN

.

.

L
I
N
E

Sacred Amongst All Others.

COPYRIGHT© | FAITHFUL SENSE™

DATE

DATE

#JustMyThoughts

<u>NOTHING</u> OUTSIDE OF YOU WILL SAVE YOU

—RALPH SMARTS

Divinely Guided & Protected.

COPYRIGHT© | FAITHFUL SENSE™

DATE

DATE

COPYRIGHT© | FAITHFUL SENSE™

#JustMyThoughts

I DON'T SUBJECT MYSELF TO ANYONE ELSE'S GOD

—

SOME SAY "HE" THEY BE LIKE "SHE"

—

I ALIGN WITHIN, AS SPIRIT THAT'S WHERE I CONNECT WITH

—

B . A . L . A . N . C . E

Grounded To Earth.

DATE

DATE

#JustMyThoughts

GROW THE "F" UP!
THERE I SAID IT ...

AS IN GROWTH WE MUST MAKE
THE CHOICES THAT RENDER PEACE
IN OUR HEARTS & MINDS AS A UNIT ...

CHOOSING TO KNOW YOU ARE:
- LOVED
  - BLESSED
    - PROTECTED

AT ALL TIMES BY AN ARMY
OF THE UNSEEN WHO HAVE BEEN
WAITING FOR YOU TO SIMPLY SAY
"SUPPORT ME" OR "I CHOOSE ME"!

RATHER THAN TO CONTINUE INNER BATTLES
OF SELF & CONVICTION, PROCLAIM THIS ...

GIVING IN TO SELF-SURRENDER,
IS NOT GIVING UP !!!

Sacred In My Purpose.

COPYRIGHT© | FAITHFUL SENSE™

DATE

DATE

#JustMyThoughts

LIVE IN YOUR TRUTH.
NOT WITH YOUR PAIN!
YES, IT'S A PART OF YOUR STORY
A SECTION IN WHICH YOU CHOOSE TO
HEAL

EMBRACE YOUR EMOTIONS!
EXPRESS YOUR TRUE FEELINGS!
RELEASE WHAT YOU'VE BEEN
DREAMING.
THINKING.
PONDERING.
QUESTIONING.
CREATIVELY
FOR SELF! & NO ONE ELSE...

Sacred In My Truth.

COPYRIGHT© | FAITHFUL SENSE™

#JustMyThoughts

LEARN TO APPRECIATE SOMEONE'S EFFORT
NO, NOTHING HAPPENS OVERNIGHT
YET BECAUSE IT WASN'T ENOUGH
FOR YOUR INSECURITY

...

DOESN'T MEAN THE NOTION WASN'T
FOUNDATION TO EXTEND THE REASSURANCE

...

WHY DISREGARD THE ENERGY
YOU INSISTED THOUGH
THEY SAY PROGRESS INCLUDES KNOWING

...

BE THAT!
TRUST THE PROCESS.
OR
THERE IS THAT MOMENT
WHEN ENOUGH IS ENOUGH

HAD ENOUGH?!

Sacred Amongst All Others.

COPYRIGHT© | FAITHFUL SENSE™

DATE

DATE

#JustMyThoughts

I NEED HER.
THOUGH I ACT LIKE I DON'T WANT WHAT I NEED,
I RELEASE IMMEDIATE THOUGHTS.
...
THIS ONE SAYS SHE'S A KEEPER
& I THINK IT WHEN I SEE THE
BEAUTY THAT'S DEEP BENEATHE.
...
WHY AM I NOT SURE IF I BELIEVE
EXACTLY WHAT IT IS I SEE?
...
COULD IT BE? YOU'RE SOME KINDA REEPER?
OH! I'M SUPPOSED TO BE THE TEACHER!
PRESENTING WHAT LOVE, PEACE & HAPPINESS
FEELS LIKE TO PLEASE HER?
DON'T TEASE HER?
...
NO NOT HER??

WELL, WHO IS SHE TO YOU ???

IMMA CREATE
A GODDESS
OUTTA YOU

Divinely Guided & Protected.

COPYRIGHT© | FAITHFUL SENSE™

DATE

DATE

#JustMyThoughts

AIN'T
NO EXPIRATON DATE
ON MY SPIRIT
SO YOU WON'T
CATCH ME
SPOILIN' YOURS

. , .

ANGELS DON'T JUST RENDER
IN THE MUNDANE OF A MOMENT!

Grounded To Earth.

COPYRIGHT© | FAITHFUL SENSE™

DATE

DATE

#JustMyThoughts

WITH A

CULTIVATING MIND.

GRATEFUL HEART.

&

VENERABLE SOUL.

—

EXPERIENCE THE FULLNESS OF YOUR BE-ING!

Sacred In My Purpose.

COPYRIGHT© | FAITHFUL SENSE™

DATE

DATE

#JustMyThoughts

IF IT DOESN'T MATTER

.,.

IF YOU DON'T CARE

.,.

IF YOU DO NOT GIVE AF

.,.

IF YOU'RE NOT BOTHERED

OR

CONCERNED ABOUT
WHAT PEOPLE THINK

&

IF YOU AREN'T STRESSIN'

...

THEN WHY TF ARE YOU
DWELLING ON YOUR
ISSUES W/ IT ?!?

STALKERS, FRENEMIES & FAKES #OOHHWHY

Sacred In My Truth.

COPYRIGHT© | FAITHFUL SENSE™

DATE

DATE

#JustMyThoughts

DEAR SHADOWS IN LOVE,

I COULD NEVER BRING MYSELF TO HATE YOU. AS I LOVED YOU INSIDE & OUT. NO NEED FOR STRESS OR DEBATE. ONCE YOU GOT IT, I BELIEVED ITS' TREASURED, IT DIDN'T END BUT SHOWIN IT DOESN'T LAST EITHER! I TOOK MY RESPECT CUZ YOU WEREN'T GIVING, TRUST & LOYALTY NAH YOU WASN'T LIVING IT... BUT I FORGIVE THE LACK THEREOF JUST COULDN'T FORGET! AFTER ALL, IN WISDOM, IT BUILT A WOMAN WELL DESERVED, NOT ON MY SOUL TO REGRET.

STRONGER & WISER TO PUSH FORWARD BEYOND YOU ALTHOUGH WE DID IT WRONG, LOVE IS THE BEST POTION. LET IT SURROUND YOU ... APPLY IT, DON'T USE IT AS A TEST! ALLOW A STEADY BEAT, DON'T RUSH, REAL LOVE BEGETS ... AND IF YOU FIND IT'S WORTH, WITH OR WITHOUT ME; KNOW THAT I'M PRAYING FOR YOUR BLESSINGS WHICH IS MY FAITHFUL HEART AT IT'S BEST!

#NOLOVELOST

JUST IN SAFE KEEPIN',
- RETURNED TO SENDER

Sacred Amongst All Others.

COPYRIGHT© | FAITHFUL SENSE™

DATE

DATE

#JustMyThoughts

I MAINTAINED
& THRIVED WITH
FAITH
AS AN ENERGY OF GOD.

—

SEEING GOD ENERGY
IN EVERYONE ELSE.

. , .

MEANWHILE "THEY"
JUST KEPT TRYNA
PROVE MY FAITH
INADEQUATE!

Divinely Guided & Protected.

COPYRIGHT© | FAITHFUL SENSE™

DATE

DATE

#JustMyThoughts

IT WASN'T THE
PARTS OF THE BIBLE
THAT I COULDN'T UNDERSTAND
THAT I UNLEARNED,
IT WAS THE PARTS
THAT I DO

., .
INNERSTAND
YOUR
BE-ING.

Grounded To Earth.

COPYRIGHT© | FAITHFUL SENSE™

DATE

DATE

www.ingramcontent.com/pod-product-compliance
Lightning Source LLC
Chambersburg PA
CBHW040421100526
44589CB00021B/2789